God's Invitation to More

A Divine Invitation to Depth, Dignity & Delight in Christ

by

Kyle Roberts and Beverly Plimpton

authorHOUSE®

AuthorHouse™
1663 Liberty Drive, Suite 200
Bloomington, IN 47403
www.authorhouse.com
Phone: 1-800-839-8640

First published by AuthorHouse 5/15/2008

ISBN: 978-1-4343-8819-3 (e)
ISBN: 978-1-4343-8821-6 (sc)
ISBN: 978-1-4343-8820-9 (hc)

Library of Congress Control Number: 2008904476

Printed in the United States of America
Bloomington, Indiana

This book is printed on acid-free paper.

To the One Who shows us the path of life;
In Whose presence is fullness of joy
At His right hand are pleasures forevermore.
To the One Who makes all things possible

Contents

Preface

With over 45 combined years of Christian experience and ministry God called us to write *God's Invitation to More* to all believers who want to trade in their complacent Christian life for the abundant life Jesus Christ promised. More often then not we have encountered Christians who live on the shore line of the Christian life. Christ called His disciples to come off the shore line and step into the deep. We long for believers to embrace Christ's invitation to the joy-filled, abundant life. This life in Christ invites each one of us to a growing intimacy and deepening personal relationship with Him.

This book is designed to invite Christians to a deeper and practical life of faith. It can be read personally or as a tool to help disciple those younger in the faith in one-on-one or in small group settings. By going through this book with another who wishes to be discipled into maturity in Christ, the discipler can identify where the disciple is in their Christian journey. This book will provide insight to the discipler to know how to pray for and encourage the younger believer.

Our heart's desire is that the content, bible reading, and questions will draw the disciple to an accurate understanding of the Christian faith and promote personal and honest reflection that will result in the following:

♦ A recognition of biblical truth

♦ An invitation to depth, dignity and delight in Christ

♦ A practical and personal process for growing in Christ

♦ And if used as a discipleship tool, a safe spiritual relationship in which personal transparency and dignity are honored with a more mature believer in Christ

Our prayer is that individuals invest in discipling a younger believer (in spiritual age) in the faith. The Bible has called us to come alongside others and help them grow in the faith and in their personal walk and intimacy with the Lord Jesus Christ.

In the New Testament the apostle Paul came alongside new and younger believers until Christ was fully formed in them. We believe this God-mandated one-on-one discipling has been virtually lost in our very busy twenty-first-century Christian lives. Without it, the entire church suffers, Christ is not glorified, and we are plagued with a church full of baby believers who are not able to fulfill God's calling on their lives.

When our stated spiritual beliefs are reflected in our everyday practical life, it is evidence that we are allowing the Spirit to lead our life into maturity in the faith. When we own what we believe, it becomes personal. Our prayer is that He may be glorified by each one of us individually and corporately as His Church, the Body of Christ.

If your heart is longing for more in the Christian faith we pray this book leads you back to your first love, Jesus Christ, the only Satisfier of your soul. We ask that you respond to His call to the deeper Christian life, we beckon you to accept God's invitation to more.

Introduction

We met at church in December 2005. Bev was on staff, in charge of the Women's Ministry. In addition to her other duties she followed up on visitors, whom the church called "prospects." My (Kyle's) initial encounters with her were at the desk on Sundays. She worked behind the information desk and was the "go to" person for sermon tapes and event details. She was so efficient and knowledgeable. I respected and appreciated her engaging smile and genuine interest to meet the needs of anyone coming up to the desk. I knew her from afar until, at her request, we met for lunch on January 22, 2007. I was pleased she invited me, but I remained guarded for two reasons. First, I was dealing with an emotional, gut-wrenching crisis in my family. My brother was in critical condition in the hospital and not expected to live. Second, I was burned out from church work and excessive busyness. The last thing I wanted was for her to ask me to do a job at the church.

Our first lunch meeting was a respectful high level exchange of history about ourselves. I let her know that I came to know Christ at the age of thirty-three. I was typical of my era in that I was a committed career woman with degrees in business and engineering. I have no children and have been married to my husband for more than twenty years. After becoming a Christian I've had an intense desire to read the Word.

Over time, God began to break me of the world's priorities and give me His priorities. My heart's growing desire and experience has been to work with women through church-based ministries and in one-on-one relationships. I want women to continually grow in intimacy with their Savior. Not to be churchy but to be Christ-like. At the time we met I was burned out from a bad case of duty-bound service in the church, had lost the intimacy in my relationship with Christ, and was in desperate need of an honest Christ-focused conversation.

Bev told me that she came to know Christ at a Christian camp at the age of twelve and was the first one saved in her family. She knew she was called into full-time service at the age of fifteen. Coming from a hard-working family business, her parents were adamant that she get a profession to support herself before going on to Bible school. They thought her "call" to full-time ministry would be fleeting. After high school Bev was sent to nursing school. She spent twenty years in campus ministries and twelve years in church-based ladies' ministries. Bev has a genuine heart for women. She has impacted countless lives with her biblical counseling, mentoring, and discipling ministries. Her passion is to invite others to a saving knowledge of Jesus Christ and to help them grow into maturity in Christ.

The first lunch was followed by another invitation from Bev to do it again the following week. She asked if I would be interested in reading and discussing a book together as we met weekly for lunch. I said yes. I thought it was an intelligent way for us to keep the conversation flowing when we ran out of things to discuss about ourselves, the Christian experience, or church life. Little did either of us know what would happen next. The book was written for Christian women who had lost their hearts along the way while performing their Christian duties and who desperately needed to hear again God's love and validation. It was the impetus to help us build a trust with each other and then express honestly, out loud and to each other, the deepest longings God had placed on our hearts. The process has had a phenomenal impact on both of us. God used it to help us recognize things we needed to repent of, seek Him more diligently, surrender our all to Him in new ways.

Both of us had a strong knowledge of, and love for, God, but somewhere along the way the intimacy got lost in duty-bound, highly rewarded, Martha-type behavior. Having been through a long dry season of disappointments and lack of authentic Christianity, it was a sheer delight to find a person who had similar longings for intimacy and growth with Christ and a desire to invite other women to the abundant life in Christ. In God's sovereign plan He brought our lives together. We learned how to build trust with each other. Having too often been a "project" to be "fixed" by well-intentioned Christian women along our path, and having been guilty of turning others into projects ourselves, we created some ground rules we could work with as we moved forward in the relationship God had given us.

We set up these ground rules:

1. God's Word would be our guide (Ps. 119:105).

2. We would value each other because we recognize that God created us uniquely for His purpose for us individually (Eph. 2:10).

3. We would respect each other's dignity (Rom. 12:10).

4. We would not try to "fix" each other or take the other on as a "project." We would let the Holy Spirit do His job (Rom. 14:10).

5. We would invite each other to freely express our hearts and minds as we discussed what God was doing in our lives (2 Tim. 1:7).

6. We would pray for each other (James 5:16).

7. We would love each other as Christ loves us (John 15:12–13).

We began to feel alive in Christ again. For the first time since our salvation we now know what it means to live a joy-filled, abundant life in Christ. We have made a deliberate choice to stay in the Word and abide in the Vine (John 15:5) so we can be sensitive to the Holy Spirit's direction, useable to others, and of profit to His kingdom. As a result of trusting and resting in God, God has made His call on our lives clear.

God has called us to write a series of books and workbooks to help others grow in intimacy with their Savior and to live authentic Christian lives. This is the first book to help you truly understand and embrace personally that God is sovereign in *your* life, that God created *you*, that God loves *you*, that God chose and gifted *you*, that God orchestrates *your* circumstances, that God has called *you* for a unique role to do His work for the kingdom of God, and that He calls *you* to worship in a growing, intimate relationship with Himself.

He is a *personal* Savior and a living God!

Chapter 1
God's Sovereignty

There was a little girl who used to watch her mother embroider. As she sat at her knee and looked up from the floor, she would ask, "What are you doing mother?" Her mother kindly replied, "I am embroidering dear." The little girl just thought it looked like a messy jumble of threads. Dark threads, light threads and all the colors in between were all she could see on the underside of the little hoop her mother held in her hand.

Her mother would smile at her, look down and sweetly say, "Go on and play for a while, and when I am finished with my embroidering, I will put you on my knee and let you see it from my side." The little girl was eager to see what her mother was so carefully and deliberately creating on her side of the hoop.

The young girl could not understand how the combination of the jumbled dark and bright threads could be anything pretty or of value. Finally, the time came when she heard her Mother's voice say, "My darling, come and sit on my knee." She ran and jumped on her mother's knee. When she saw the top side of the hoop it made her gasp in amazement. She exclaimed, "What a beautiful sunset!" She could not believe such beauty and purpose could be created out of a messy, entangled bunch of dark and light threads woven together.

Then her mother said to her, "My dear, from underneath it did look messy and jumbled, but you did not realize that there was a pre-drawn master plan on the top. I was following a master design."

Many times we have looked up to our Heavenly Father and said, "Father, what are You doing?"

He has answered, "I am embroidering your life."

1

We say, "But it looks like a mess to me. It seems so jumbled. The threads seem so dark. Why can't they all be bright? Please give me more bright threads."

The Father seems to tell us, "'My child, you go about your business of doing My business, and one day I will bring you to Heaven and put you on My knee and you will see the perfect master plan from My side."

Why is it important to discuss the sovereignty of God? Scripture has many verses that say our all-wise, all-knowing, omnipotent God reigns in realms beyond our comprehension to bring about a plan beyond our ability. When we embrace the doctrinal truth of God's sovereignty and apply it to our personal lives it enables us to rest in Him, trust in Him, and rely on Him regardless of our circumstances.

Most of us would agree that we believe God is sovereign. We believe God is the Creator and Ruler of the universe, but when it comes to our personal lives, well, that's another matter. But what does it mean to say that God is sovereign?

> We mean the supremacy of God, the kingship of God, the godhood of God. To say that God is sovereign is to declare that God is God. To say that God is sovereign is to declare that he is the Most High, doing according to his will in the army of Heaven, and among the inhabitants of the earth, so that none can stay his hand or say unto him what doest thou? (Dan. 4:35). To say that God is sovereign is to declare that he is the Almighty, the Possessor of all power in heaven and earth, so that none can defeat his counsels, thwart his purpose, or resist his will (Ps. 115:3). To say that God is sovereign is to declare that he is "The Governor among the nations" (Ps. 22:28), setting up kingdoms, overthrowing empires, and determining the course of dynasties as pleaseth him best. To say that God is sovereign is to declare that he is the "Only Potentate, the King of kings, and Lord of lords" (1 Tim. 6:15). Such is the God of the Bible.

The sovereignty of the God of Scripture is absolute, irresistible, and infinite. When we say that God is sovereign we affirm his right to govern the universe, which he has made for his own glory, just as he pleases. We affirm that his right is the right of the Potter over the clay, i.e., that he may mold that clay into whatsoever form he chooses, fashioning out of the same lump one vessel unto honour and another unto dishonour. We affirm that he is under no rule or law outside of his own will and nature, that God is a law unto himself, and that he is under no obligation to give an account of his matters to any.[1]

According to the Bible, God is in control of everything past, present and future. Today He is sovereign over our universe, our world, our country, our town, and our individual lives. Scripture supports this throughout the Old and New Testaments:

♦ When Moses was chosen by God to lead the Israelites out of Egypt, he said to God, "'O my Lord, I am not eloquent, neither before nor since You have spoken to Your servant; but I am slow of speech and slow of tongue.' So the Lord said to him, 'Who has made man's mouth? Or who makes the mute, the deaf, the seeing, or the blind? Have not I, the Lord? Now therefore, go, and I will be with your mouth and teach you what you shall say'" (Exod. 4:10–12).

♦ "Yours, O Lord, is the greatness, the power and the glory, the victory and the majesty; For all that is in heaven and in earth is Yours; Yours is the kingdom, O Lord, and You are exalted as head over all" (1 Chron. 29:11).

♦ He formed you in your mother's womb (Ps. 139:13–14).

♦ When Jesus healed the man blind from birth, the disciples asked Him, "Who sinned, this man or his parents, that he was born blind?" The Lord Jesus told them, "Neither this man nor his parents sinned, but that the works of God should be revealed in him" (John 9:2–3).

God formed you in your mother's womb, placed you in the family you were born into, chose the color of your hair, designed the shape of your body, and gave you your unique DNA. He has equipped you with certain talents, mental and physical abilities. And if you are born again in Christ, He has also given you gifts to fulfill your unique place in the body of Christ for His eternal purposes on earth (1 Corinthians 12).

If you are like me and many people I have spoken with, you agree with the verses in the Word of God that clearly demonstrate the sovereignty of God. Yet when we honestly look at ourselves, we often see a huge disconnect. At first glance it is not apparent. But a deliberate closer look reveals that our view of ourselves, our attitudes toward life, and the choices we make are inconsistent with our mental assent to the sovereignty of God.

In the center of Main Street in Enterprise, Alabama, stands one of the strangest monuments in the world. It's a memorial to an insect! Handsomely carved in stone is the likeness of a boll weevil. Many believe that divine providence was involved in the circumstances that led to the erection of this unusual statue. In early plantation days almost everyone in the community raised cotton. But as the years rolled on, a serious pestilence infested the area in the form of a small beetle that punctured the boll of the cotton plant. As a result, it became almost impossible to bring a season's growth to maturity. George Washington Carver, along with several other scientists, became deeply concerned about the situation and began intensive studies to see if any substitute crop could be grown in that part of the country. Raising peanuts was the answer, for they could be planted and harvested with very little loss. In time, cotton gins were forgotten in that region, and it became known as the peanut center of the world. Soon the farmers' profits far exceeded what they had earned from their best cotton yield. In the end, they realized that the destructive insect they had feared had actually triggered the research that brought them prosperity.

The Lord often allows trials to unsettle our lives for a blessed purpose. Perhaps we are trying to grow cotton when we should be raising peanuts.

If so, the delays and disappointments we experience are just the gracious "boll weevils" sent to redirect us so that we will plant the crop of God's choosing.

∞ Live your life *knowing* ∞
God is Sovereign

Chapter 1 – God's Sovereignty

Make it Personal

1. What is your opinion of the family you were born into (wonderful, difficult, unfortunate, got dealt a bad hand, wish it were different, etc.)?

2. What is your view of the circumstances you have lived through (i.e., social/financial status, home life, physical and mental abilities, education level, spouse, children, etc.)?

3. How would you summarize your current situation?

4. Where is God in the situations and circumstances described above?

5. God typically uses trials to draw us to Him. After our salvation He uses them to help us die to self and become more Christ-like. He also uses our past to shape our calling and our future for His glory. Have you let God use your circumstances to shape you?

    If so, how? If not, why?

6. List five things in your life which are most important to you (relationships, passions, work, etc.).

7. The story of Joseph is recorded in Genesis 37–48. Joseph's response and attitude toward his brothers, who had greatly wronged him, comes in Genesis 45:8: "So now it was not you who sent me here, but God; and He has made me a father to Pharaoh, and lord of all his house, and a ruler throughout all the land of Egypt." Again he responded to his brothers in Genesis 50:20, "But as for you, you meant evil against me; but God meant it for good." How does this story relate to your story?

8. Sovereignty draws us, like Joseph, to come to conclusions about God's role in our lives. How would you describe your view of God's role in your life to date?

9. What changes would you like to make to be more available to God and the unique plan He has for your life?

10. "For I know the thoughts that I think toward you, says the Lord, thoughts of peace and not of evil, to give you a future and a hope" (Jer. 29:11). Consider this verse. What does this mean for your life?

Chapter 2
God Created You

"You are worthy, O Lord, to receive glory and honor and power; for You created all things, and by Your will they exist and were created." (Rev. 4:11)

God created you at the exact time in history He planned before the foundation of the world and placed you into the family He chose for you. He gave you your distinctive personality, talents, and looks. Even more, in His sovereignty He has orchestrated your circumstances, planned the people and places in your life, and allowed the trials of life to draw you to Him through salvation and to help you become more Christ-like.

You may ask why we even need to address the fact that God created you. Isn't it obvious? It is obvious intellectually and we believe it spiritually, but emotionally we don't seem to own the thought that God created *me*. Why did He create you and me? He created you because He wants a personal relationship with *you* and He has a sovereign plan for *your* life. He is a very personal God who wants an ongoing, intimate relationship with His human creation, and that includes you uniquely and personally. Ravi Zacharias stated it well in his book *The Grand Weaver*.

> I believe God intervenes in the lives of *every one of us*. He speaks to us in different ways and at different times so that we may know He is the author of our very personality. And He wants us to know He has a calling for each of us, designed to fulfill each individual's uniqueness. That is why John and Peter and a host of others, in the end, willingly paid the ultimate price, even as they sought God's power and presence in those "dark

nights of the soul." In fact, I believe more matters to God in our lives then we normally pause to think about. We may not fully understand His design as it takes shape, but we should not conclude that His design lacks a directing plan.[1]

We see the purpose of God creating many ordinary, imperfect people who became great biblical characters of faith because the Bible tells us of the impact of their lives retrospectively. Noah, Abraham, Isaac, Jacob, Sarah, Joseph, Rahab, Gideon, Barak, Samson, Jephthah, Esther, Ruth, David, Samuel, the prophets, John the Baptist, Mary, Jesus' disciples, and the apostle Paul, to name a few. Each of these people lived by faith and obeyed the call of God on their lives. Even now we are called to fulfill God's sovereign plan in our individual lives using the unique personality, talent, and spiritual gifts God has given to each of us.

Just as the biblical characters have a story, you have a story, *your* life story. Reviewing your life and looking at your story will help you see God's sovereign authorship of your life. When you look at, recount, and write your life story you will begin to recognize how much God values you. You will also begin to see the circumstances God has used to shape you and prepare you for the future He has planned for you. He wants to use your past to shape your future redemptive story. It all can be used to glorify Him and enable you to work to further His kingdom on this earth.

Through the process of writing your life story you can begin to fully recognize and own your story. Then you begin to be a co-author with God in your future.

You may be skeptical at the overgrown path back through your stories and wonder if it's even worth it. After all, shouldn't we follow the old adage and let sleeping dogs lie? Dan Allender and Lisa Fann wrote a great workbook entitled, *To Be Told* that provides a process to use to write one's stories. They astutely point out the litany of reasons not to write our story that race through our minds.

Many reluctant pilgrims will argue, *I already walked through that. The past is the past; there's no reason to rehash it. What benefit could possibly come from walking back into those stories?* Too often we tell our stories poorly. We tell our stories without curiosity and create only boredom. We tell them without honesty and add another layer of shellac to an already idealized past. We tell them without gentleness and weave tales of vengeance against ourselves and others. By telling our stories poorly, we dishonor them and mire ourselves in anger and contempt. No wonder the reluctant pilgrims argue so vehemently against looking at the past. Often they have struggled and toiled to leave the past behind. What could possibly induce someone to sully the present by dredging up old stories?[2]

The stories of our life affect us unconsciously or consciously. Who we are today is a direct result of the past events in our life and how we responded to those events. As Dan Allender and Lisa Fann said, "It's up to us to decide whether we'll be passive recipients or active agents in the shaping of our lives."

I must confess that I have always been reluctant to rehash my past. I saw no value in it and I comfortably tucked this opinion, along with my past, neatly away in the corner of my Christian mind, believing it would be too self-centered and self-focused to look back. My time could be much better spent focusing on Christ and others. I was startled when Bev invited me to go through the process of writing and telling our stories to each other; I was tentative and fearful. But to my amazement, the process had the opposite effect of what I expected. I began to see how much God's hand had been and was shaping my life.

As I stopped and truly looked at the joys, the sorrows, the shame, the abandonment, the reconciliation, and the redemption stories of my life, I began to realize that my life was truly a part of God's deliberate design and His beautiful tapestry. Even when I had made wrong choices and suffered the consequences, God brought redemption. I became much more thankful to God for circumstances I had forgotten or avoided from my past because I could see much more of God's purpose for me and His faithfulness to me. I began to feel whole and valid. I began to own and embrace the woman God made me to be.

After reading *To Be Told*, Bev and I began writing responses to the questions in the *To Be Told* workbook. We wrote on our own and met weekly to go over the stories we had written. It took a lot of courage and honesty. It was a trust-building process for both of us. Often our lives are so busy that they are a blur. We rarely take time to reflect on our lives and what God is doing in us. Instead, we react to the constant demands and urgencies of life. The risk of stopping seems too great. It could cost us dearly in disappointed expectations of others or ourselves. It is much easier to stay on task and not take the seemingly difficult path back through our stories.

Many times Christ called His disciples to come apart from the activities of life. He invites us to rest (Matt. 11:28–30; Mark 6:31) and to abide in Him. He does not call us to a life of constant activity but a life of activity combined with Sabbath rest, worship, simple trust in Him, and obedience to His Word. As we take time to reflect on what He had done and is doing through the circumstances He orchestrates in our life, our relationships with people, and our relationship with Him, we find life-changing refreshment for our soul. King David in the Psalms routinely reflected on what God had done. He saw His hand in every aspect of his circumstances and his life. In and through the stories of David's life he petitioned, praised, repented, rejoiced, and let his heart be known both to himself and to His God.

God values the uniqueness of each individual story. The Bible is full of detailed stories that include both the lovely and the harsh realities of the lives of individuals He created. As you reflect on and, hopefully, write your story, it won't be easy. You will revisit stories of love, betrayal, shame, abandonment, peace, injustice, and redemption. It will lead to moments of great joy and deep sorrow. But as you look back you will be able to see God's redemptive hand and purpose in your life. I pray that you choose to reflect on your life and allow God to use it to be all He created *you* to be for His eternal purpose.

∞ Live your life *knowing* ∞
God created you

Chapter 2 - God Created You

Make it Personal

1. In biblical times children were often given names that reflected their nature and personality. What is the meaning of your name? Briefly describe your personality and nature.

2. God changed Abram's name (honored father) to Abraham (father of many), Sarai's (my princess) to Sarah (princess), and Jacob's (deceitful one) to Israel (God contended or champion of God). As they stepped into fulfilling God's sovereign purpose for their lives, their names were changed to reflect their purpose. God promises us that we will be given a new name in eternity. What would you like yours to be?

3. Write a sentence for each scene from your life that seemed to have a significant impact on you.

4. What have been your most prevalent thought patterns about yourself and your life?

5. Can you trace back the source of your thought patterns about yourself? Give examples.

6. God uses our past to shape us and use us for His specific purposes. (For example, people who have been lonely or hurt often have a special awareness and heart to reach out to those who have been abandoned and hurt.) As you reflect on your past, what could be used for His glory in serving or ministering to others?

7. Do you believe that God has a created you and called you to a unique role to live for Him on this earth?

If so, what do you suspect it is?

Chapter 3
God Loves You

"To know the love of Christ which passes knowledge; that you may be filled with all the fullness of God." (Eph. 3:19)

How do I know that God loves me? "John 3:16 states that *God so loved the world that He gave His only begotten Son* to redeem us and reconcile us to Himself. Through His redemption plan of salvation, the Spirit of God has brought me into intimate contact with the true Person of God Himself."[1]

> But God, who is rich in mercy, because of His great love with which He loved us, even when we were dead in trespasses, made us alive together with Christ (by grace you have been saved), and raised us up together, and made us sit together in the heavenly places in Christ Jesus, that in the ages to come He might show the exceeding riches of His grace in His kindness toward us in Christ Jesus. (Eph. 2:4–7)

I had been growing in my Christian faith for sixteen years before I truly accepted and began to know that God loved *me*. Of course I believed it because the Bible said it, and originally it was His love shown in John 3:16 that called me to surrender my life to Jesus Christ at salvation. But it was an intellectual knowledge. I didn't own it emotionally or practically. My life was filled with trying to please God and my fellow Christians. I looked like a good Christian woman on the outside. But on the inside I was plagued with thoughts of inadequacy, insecurity, and a to-do list with more on it than I could humanly do so that I could feel I was pleasing God.

Through a series of deep trials God had been breaking me of all those little gods and things in my life. It was a very difficult and lonely time. It wasn't until later that I realized it was for my good. He wanted those things removed so He could fill me with Himself and His purpose for me. I had been led to read Ephesians daily for quite some time, and then God laid on my heart to personalize it as if He wrote it to me. I wrote all the Scriptures relating to God's love for me on a notepad and then read them to myself every day for a month. Amazingly, God has given me a confidence and knowledge to know He loves me.

The book of Ephesians, especially chapters 1–3, clearly outlines His personal love and plan for His children on this earth and in eternity.

The points below are personalized to encourage you to read them as if God wrote them to you. Embrace and own the riches Christ Jesus has given you:

- He blessed me with all spiritual blessings in heavenly places in Christ.

- He chose me in Him before the foundation of the world that I should be holy and without blame before Him in love.

- He predestined me into the adoption by Jesus Christ Himself according to the good pleasure of His will.

- He has made me accepted in the beloved.

- He has abounded toward me in all wisdom and understanding.

- I have obtained an inheritance, being predestined according to His purpose.

- He sealed me with the Holy Spirit of promise that I may know what is the hope of His calling, and what are the riches of glory of His inheritance in the saints, and what is the exceeding greatness of His power to me according to the working of His mighty power.

- God, who is rich in mercy and great love with which He loved me, even when I was dead in sins, has made me alive with the other saints with Christ. By grace I am saved. He has raised us up together; and made us sit together in the heavenly places in Christ Jesus. In the ages to come He might show the exceeding riches of His grace in His kindness toward me though Christ.

- By grace I am saved through faith; it is not of me, it is the gift of God. Not of works lest I should boast.

- I am His workmanship created in Christ Jesus unto good works, which God hath before ordained that I should walk in them.

- He is my peace.

- I have access by one Spirit to the Father.

- I, along with other believers, am no more a stranger and foreigner but a fellow citizen with the saints and of the household of God. We are built upon the foundation of the apostles and prophets, Jesus Christ Himself being the chief cornerstone.

- I am part of the holy temple of the Lord—a habitation of God through the Spirit.

- I am a fellow heir, and of the same body, and partaker of His promise in Christ, the gospel.

- I have boldness and access with confidence by faith in Him.

- I pray according to the riches of His glory to be strengthened with might by His Spirit in the inner man.

- That Christ may dwell in my heart by faith, being rooted and grounded in love, I may be able to comprehend what is the breadth and length and depth and height and to know the love of Christ, which passeth knowledge, that I might be filled with all the fullness of God.

"Who shall separate us from the love of Christ?" (Rom. 8:35)

Nothing can separate us from the love of Christ. Even though He loves us, He does not keep His children immune from trouble, trials, and tribulation. He promises that He will be with us in the trouble. Psalm 91:15 says, "He shall call upon me and I will answer him: I will be with him in trouble, I will honor him." No matter how difficult the circumstance or seemingly unbearable the trial, He will always love us and give us power to endure and overcome. His Word says we are more than conquerors through Him that loved us (Rom. 8:37). The apostle Paul was referring to things that are dangerously real (tribulation, distress, persecution, famine, nakedness, peril, or death). He said we are more than conquerors in the midst of them, not because of any ability or special power on our part but because none of them affects our essential relationship with God in Jesus Christ.

We never welcome tribulation in our lives with open arms. But we are promised that God will never leave us or forsake us and that He will always love us no matter how hard the trial. We should not allow tribulations or the cares of this world to separate us from remembering that God loves us. He not only loves us; He is using the trial to grow us and make us more conformed to His image through the trial.

Do we believe God's love will continue to hold us fast, even when everyone and everything around us seems to be saying that His love is a lie, and that there is no such thing as justice?

Can we not only believe in the love of God but also be "more than conquerors," even while we are being mistreated or ignored or when we feel unloved by others?

Oswald Chambers says, "Either Jesus Christ is a deceiver, having deceived even Paul, or else some extraordinary thing happens to someone who holds on to the love of God when the odds are totally against him. Logic is silenced in the face of each of these things which come against him. Only one thing can account for it—the *love of God in Christ Jesus.*"[2]

God's love and God's holiness go hand in hand. God is holy. He cannot have sin in His presence. When man sinned in the Old Testament the only way he could have fellowship with God was after he killed an unblemished animal and offered a blood sacrifice for the temporary covering of sin. The Old Testament sacrifices for sin were a fore shadow of the ultimate Perfect Lamb, Jesus Christ, who became sin for us at the cross (2 Cor. 5:21) and imputed His righteousness to us to redeem us to a Holy God. In the New Covenant (Testament) we are told that God so loved us that He sent His son to die on the cross to reconcile us to a Holy God. What happened to sin at the cross? It lost its power in all of those who surrender their life to Jesus Christ as the Lord and Savior of their life. God sent His Son to die on the cross to redeem us from the penalty of sin (hell), the power of sin (we choose to live each day abiding in the Spirit or sinful flesh), and the presence of sin (no more sin in heaven).

What an awesome love it is that God would demonstrate His love to us through the agony of Jesus Christ at the cross. As His redeemed ones we can have a relationship with a Holy God and He with us because He sees Christ's righteousness in us through the blood of Jesus Christ. God created us to have relationship with Him. After the fall in the Garden of Eden He provided a temporary covering for sin then as promised throughout the Old Testament and fulfilled in the New Testament, through Jesus Christ. Through His once for all atoning death on the cross, God made a way to show His love to us and have relationship with us, His beloved, created, and chosen ones.

∞ Live your life *knowing* ∞
God loves you

Chapter 3 - God Loves You

Make it Personal

1. As you read the first three chapters of Ephesians and consider the cross do you comprehend the love God has for you?

    Explain.

2. Since you have become a Christian has your love for Christ increased, decreased, or stayed the same?

3. What circumstances in your life have caused you to doubt God's love toward you?

4. In your own words, how does the love of God and the Holiness of God get reconciled at the cross?

5. The bible says if we love God we will obey Him and we will delight to do His will. When you meditate on the love of God towards you, what does it compel you to do?

6. Knowing our earthly relationships can affect our view of our heavenly Father, how do you view your heavenly Father (i.e. harsh, distant, loving, kind, unavailable, etc.)?

7. Read Romans 8:35–39. How does this apply in your life?

Chapter 4
God Chose and Gifted You

"Blessed be the God and Father of our Lord Jesus Christ, who has blessed us with every spiritual blessing in the heavenly places in Christ, just as He chose us in Him before the foundation of the world, that we should be holy and without blame before Him in love." (Eph. 1:3–4)

"Before I formed you in the womb I knew you" (Jer. 1:5). Our minds have great difficulty comprehending how much we mean to God. We often don't understand or embrace the dignity that is ours when we believe He formed each one of us in our mother's womb, called us to life, and chose us to come to salvation and redemption in Christ. Beyond that, He gifted us to empower and enable us to do the work He chose for us here on earth.

The world will tell us that we evolved or just happened to come into being with no Master or master plan. But we know from Scripture that we were chosen by God to exist. Before time began God chose each one of us and this choice was deliberate. His divine providence placed us in a time and state of life that would call us to fulfill our part of His plan in the kingdom of God.

He gave each of us our unique personality, special talents, gifts and natural virtues. These traits lived out through our redemption and in the power of the Holy Spirit point us toward a deeper knowledge of Himself. He calls us to a deep relationship with Himself and calls us to serve His people. He calls us to walk in the Spirit so we can worship Him in Spirit and in truth. We are divinely equipped to fulfill the purpose and work He has chosen for us.

At redemption He filled us with His Holy Spirit, God in us. He warns us through His Word and His Spirit of things we must avoid and calls us to those things we must pursue. He warns us to avoid sin and any situation or people that could lead us into sin. Much like loving parents keep their children from playing in the street, He keeps us from harm when we obey Him. He chose us to a life of peace and joy. He calls us to pursue and praise Christ and meditate on those virtuous things listed in Philippians 4:8, whatever things are true, honest, just, pure, lovely, and of good report. In the rigors of everyday life it seems hard to find those positive attributes to think about. At closer glance you will see that the list in Philippians summarizes the nature of our living Savior, the Lord Jesus Christ. When we meditate on Him we are led to praise and worship Him for His truth, honesty, justice, purity, loveliness, and goodness in all of life.

Christ said several times that His sheep hear His voice. Specifically in John 10:3–4, He said, "To Him the doorkeeper opens, and the sheep hear His voice, and He calls His own sheep by name and leads them out. And when He brings out His own sheep, He goes before them; and the sheep follow Him, for they know His voice." Further in the book of John, after the resurrection, when Jesus appeared to Mary Magdalene she thought He was the gardener. She did not recognize the resurrected Christ until He called her name—"Mary!"

What was it that made her recognize Jesus? It must have been that she heard the Shepherd's voice because she was called to be one of His sheep. Her name was written in the Book of Life at redemption and pronounced by God before she was born. God created and formed her in her mother's womb. She was born into sin, but she sorrowed over her Savior's death and was redeemed from sin by the resurrected Savior. The first time her name was pronounced, her birth was decreed. The second time she came to physical life. The third time it called her to the second birth, and now after the resurrection, it called her to recognize God in the Spirit. When man calls us by name it is meaningful and we respond, but when God pronounces it, it gives life, divine power, grace, and abundant joy.

When Jesus said, "Saul, Saul, why do you persecute Me?" the man was blinded, transformed, and renamed Paul. Paul was given divine power and changed dramatically from a Christian-killing Pharisee to one of the most important apostles. He was then used as an instrument of God to bring many to salvation and growth in Christ, both in his lifetime and all future generations. God used Paul as the instrument to write a good portion of the New Testament.

A dead man arose when Jesus said, "Lazarus come forth." When He changed the name of Simon ("Listening") to Peter ("Rock"), He gave a specific work for him—to take the good news to the Jews—and equipped him with power from on high. How incredibly wonderful that God calls your name and mine and gives us His mercy, grace, and divine power to change and respond to His love.

Often we mistake God's silence for absence and neglect. But God has never forsaken or left any of us. He chose us in Him before the foundation of the world. He placed us in our mothers' wombs and brought us up in the family and circumstances He appointed. God chose you and sovereignly orchestrated your circumstances to equip you and make you a robust saint useable for His kingdom work. He wants to use your distinctive personality, talents, circumstances, the trials and hardships of your past that have shaped you, and the spiritual gifts He has given you. The Christians who are most helpful to others are those who have allowed God to have His will be done in their life, those who have allowed Him to break, make, and mold them in into His image. He does this through the trial of fire to burn off the dross (sin) in our lives. A line from the famous hymn, *Spirit of the Living God*, says it best, "break me, melt me, mold me, fill me."

"My frame was not hidden from You, when I was made in secret, and skillfully wrought in the lowest parts of the earth" (Ps. 139:15). He knows every aspect of us from our formation until now. Only our Father truly knows us as we are. No human being even comes close to knowing us like God knows us. We don't even approach knowing ourselves like God knows us. That is why He asks us to trust Him; He alone knows what is best for us. God is not surprised by anything we've done or any thought we have had. He knows every aspect of us—our creation, life, wrong choices, right choices, temperament, capabilities, and characteristics. He knew the crosses that we would have and will have at every juncture of our life. He knows how each cross is uniquely designed for shaping and conforming us into His image. Like King David, our hearts' desire can be expressed from Psalm 17:15, "As for me, I will see your face in righteousness; I shall be satisfied when I awake in Your likeness."

God the Father looks forward to the day He will see Himself clearly mirrored in us. He earnestly seeks us and anticipates our choosing Him above all things, knowing what abundant joy and wondrous glory that ultimate choice will give us. He sees the holiness we could obtain, the heart of humility and dependence on Him that could guide us, and the simplicity and joy in the life that could be ours when we are completely dependent on Him. He sees the tears that His love can gently wipe away, the times He holds us by His right hand to keep us on the narrow path. He forgives us when we stumble. He has seen our wrong choices and grieved over our unnecessary pain. He seeks us and calls us to repentance and reconciliation for His glory and our best good. Yes, He knows our past, our present, and our future and He still loves us!

> *"You will show me the path of life; in Your*
> *presence is fullness of joy; at Your right hand are*
> *pleasures forevermore."* (Psalm 16:11)

Because of our sin nature we struggle with believing God cares for us and loves us as much as His Word declares. Like the woman at the well, we are surprised that Jesus Christ would pursue and choose us. When we don't see ourselves from God's perspective we pridefully view ourselves as better than we are and seek value in everything but Him.

But often pride shows itself in a not so obvious way, especially in women. We are consumed with *self*-consciousness and have such a low opinion of ourselves that we don't truly believe we are valued by God and therefore don't hear or heed His calling for us beyond our salvation. The sad result is that our delight in His love is short-lived. We reserve our expression of love for God as an act of gratitude after some blessing or answer to prayer has been received. But how often do we meditate on God's love for us—not only now but before the foundation of the world?

Calvary love is beyond our comprehension. *And Can it Be That I Should Gain*, written by Charles Wesley in the 18th century, expresses this overwhelming love beautifully and biblically in his great hymn:

And Can it Be That I Should Gain?

And can it be that I should gain
an interest in the Savior's blood!
Died he for me? who caused his pain!
For me? who him to death pursued?
Amazing love! How can it be
that thou, my God, shouldst die for me?
Amazing love! How can it be
that thou, my God, shouldst die for me?

'Tis mystery all: th' Immortal dies!
Who can explore his strange design?
In vain the firstborn seraph tries
to sound the depths of love divine.
'Tis mercy all! Let earth adore;
let angel minds inquire no more.
'Tis mercy all! Let earth adore;
let angel minds inquire no more.

He left his Father's throne above
(so free, so infinite his grace!),

emptied himself of all but love,
and bled for Adam's helpless race.
'Tis mercy all, immense and free,
for O my God, it found out me!
'Tis mercy all, immense and free,
for O my God, it found out me!

Long my imprisoned sprit lay,
fast bound in sin and nature's night;
thine eye diffused a quickening ray;
I woke, the dungeon flamed with light;
my chains fell off, my heart was free,
I rose, went forth, and followed thee.
My chains fell off, my heart was free,
I rose, went forth, and followed thee.

No condemnation now I dread;
Jesus, and all in him, is mine;
alive in him, my living Head,
and clothed in righteousness divine,
bold I approach th' eternal throne,
and claim the crown, through Christ my own.
Bold I approach th' eternal throne,
and claim the crown, through Christ my own.

Words: Charles Wesley, 1739 (Acts 16:26)

In light of His great love demonstrated in His choosing us, creating us, calling us, and redeeming us how do we respond? We have a great mission to fulfill, a part to play, and a place to fill in His kingdom. We have a God-given role to perform and a work to accomplish. We are vitally important to God and an integral part of salvation history.

We can truthfully say each of us affects the world for good or bad. We have significant influence for good when we use the gifts God has given us for His glory. Conversely, we don't have the impact or influence God intends for us when we don't believe He chose us as His Word claims, or see ourselves from God's perspective and love others as He has loved us. We are chosen by God no matter how insignificant we view our role, how lowly our position, how unknown our contribution. Each one of us is uniquely gifted by God and we all leave a legacy in some way upon this world. No wonder He chooses us with great care and determines our course with His infinite love. What a gift He has given us!

> *"But each one has his own gift from God, one in*
> *this manner and another in that."*
> (1 Cor. 7:7)

God has sovereignly given each one of us one or more spiritual gifts. These gifts are given to us so that we are able to minister to others in God's power. Among others, the gifts include:

Enabling gifts are given to all Christians to help us use our specific task gifts:

♦ Faith (Rom. 1:11; 1 Cor. 12:9)

♦ Knowledge (1 Cor. 12:8)

♦ Wisdom (1 Cor. 12:8)

♦ Discernment (1 Cor. 12:10)

We also may have motivational gifts:

♦ Prophecy (Rom. 12:6; 1 Cor. 14:3)

♦ Teaching (Rom. 12:7)

♦ Exhortation (Rom. 12:8)

♦ Shepherding (Eph. 4:11)

♦ Showing Mercy (Rom. 12:8)

◆ Ministering (Rom. 12:7)

◆ Helping (1 Cor. 12:28)

◆ Giving (Rom. 12:8)

◆ Ruling (Rom. 12:8)

◆ Governing (1 Cor. 12:28)

◆ Evangelism (Eph. 4:11)

◆ Hospitality (1 Pet. 4:9)

According to 1 Corinthians 7:7, quoted above, every Christian has at least one spiritual gift. Romans 12:3–8 calls each one of us to know and exercise the gift(s) God has given us. Many of us underestimate ourselves and fail to know or exercise the gift we were given by God. However, since these passages clearly indicate that no Christian is excluded, we must be diligent to know the gift(s) God has given us and to exercise it/them in love and humility to edify the body of Christ.

I was leading a women's Bible study on the spiritual gifts in our church one evening, and I was delighted to see a number of visitors whom I had not met. As we separated into smaller groups, my group had fifteen people. To get acquainted we went around the circle of women and each told how long she had been a believer. I always like learning from older women of the faith, and I was eager to hear from the three visiting women who were seventy-plus years of age. The maturity levels of the women ranged from new believers to those saved for many decades.

As we went through the study on spiritual gifts there was good interaction and discussion among us. At the end of the study I asked each woman to tell what she thought her spiritual gifts were, and if she wasn't sure to give her passion in life. I was saddened to hear the responses. Almost no one knew her God-given gift(s). Even more, the women who were saved for more than fifty years and in their seventies did not have any idea what their gifts were.

On the other end of the spectrum we may learn the gifts and decide what ours are and, without much prayer, discernment, humility, or love, we launch into "service" for God, running roughshod over our brothers and sisters in Christ. In the end, not much edifying of the saints was accomplished and we end up doing God's work in the flesh. A similar result happens when churches call us to duty and service and we volunteer to do whatever they need done, often out of guilt or needing man's approval, and not out of calling or giftedness.

Duty is only a substitute
for love of God and other people.
The Collected Letters of C.S. Lewis, Volume III

It is important to take time to pray over what God has chosen and uniquely gifted you to do. It is vital to the body of Christ that we examine all requests of our time and ability prayerfully and in light of Scripture until we have discernment from God, rather than saying yes because there is a need or saying no because we are too busy or not interested. Our willingness to serve increases along with our awareness that God invites us to *particular* activities, not just to activity. C. S. Lewis said in one of his letters, "I now see that I spent most of my life in doing neither what I ought or what I liked."[1]

Christ told the disciples to preach the gospel to all people throughout the world, to let others know the good news that they could be saved by faith in Jesus Christ. But He forbad them to go immediately. He told them to wait until they had power from on high. We too must wait on God's direction and power in our lives. He chose and gifted us personally and uniquely to do His work, in His timing and power.

God has a much bigger plan for His children and how we work together to accomplish His work on this earth. We can't see the full picture, but we can be faithful in what He has uniquely chosen and equipped us with his gifts to do. In eternity we will each stand before the Bema Seat of Christ. "The Bema Seat is described in 1 Corinthians 3:12–15.

Now if anyone builds on this foundation with gold, silver, precious stones, wood, hay, straw, each one's work will become clear; for the Day will declare it, because it will be revealed by fire; and the fire will test each one's work, of what sort it is. If anyone's work which he has built on it endures, he will receive a reward. If anyone's work is burned, he will suffer loss; but he himself will be saved, yet so as through fire.

Your gold, silver, and costly stones are works done for the glory of God, with the right motive, and in dependence upon the power of the Holy Spirit. In Revelation 22:12, Jesus Christ declares, "And behold, I am coming quickly, and My reward is with Me, to give to every one according to his work."[2]

∞ **Live your life *knowing*** ∞
God chose & gifted you

Chapter 4 - God Chose and Gifted You

Make it Personal

1. Do you believe that God chose and gifted you?

   Why?

2. Describe your experiences serving God (joyful, dutiful, obedient, in the Spirit or not, etc.).

3. What do you think your spiritual gifts are?

4. Would you say your Christian life has been spent doing what God has called and gifted *you* specifically to do?

   If not, why?

5. When you stand before Christ at the Bema seat to give an account of your time on earth, what words do you think you will hear from Him?

6. If you are uncomfortable with your response to question 5, what changes would you like to make in your life so you can hear Him say, "Well done, My good and faithful servant"?

7. Which of these things do you need to turn away from (repent of) before God?

- ♦ Doing God's work in the flesh versus being led by the Spirit

- ♦ Not spending time in the Word or prayer even to know what God wants for your life

- ♦ Not doing anything with the gifts God has given you (burying your talents)

- ♦ Being active in the church out of guilt and/or to look good in man's eyes

- ♦ Having a prideful attitude about yourself and your abilities

- ♦ Not praying before responding to requests for your time or talents

- ♦ Wasting time with the cares of the world and not living for the Kingdom of God

- ♦ Not protecting your time with Him and delighting in your relationship with Him

If God has convicted you of something else that's not in the list, be sure to mention it below also.

Dear God, I repent of the following in my life . . .

Chapter 5
God Orchestrates Your Circumstances

"Trust in the Lord with all your heart, and lean not on your own understanding; In all your ways acknowledge Him, and He shall direct your paths." (Prov. 3:5–6)

Bev Plimpton was raised in a non-Christian home with no encouragement from her family to help her grow after her salvation at the age of twelve. In fact, her mother was openly hostile to the news of her daughter's salvation. Her mother told her, "I would rather you come home and tell me you were pregnant than a Christian." Nonetheless, God never left her alone. He provided Christian neighbors who took her to church on Sundays. It was a church of about three hundred people who, for the most part, seemed disinterested and unexcited about Bev's salvation or baptism.

Later that year a woman named Amy came to visit the church, and then Bev's life would be forever changed. Amy spoke about discipleship for children and the importance of Christians helping younger Christians grow in the faith. Bev became aware of what discipleship was. Bev was so affected by Amy's talk that she went up afterward and asked Amy to help her grow.

Amy was a faithful, godly woman in her sixties; Bev was a teenager. For three years Amy drove two hours a week to come and disciple Bev. When Bev was in the tenth grade she received an assignment to write an essay on the three things she wanted to do in life. Without hesitation she wrote her heart's desire of being called to be in full-time ministry for Him. She knew the call of God on her life.

Bev continued to grow richly in Christ from her weekly discipleship meetings with Amy. Her parents started feeling threatened by the Christian influence Amy had on Bev. In her sophomore year, Bev's parents forbad Bev from having any future meetings with Amy. Bev's desire was to attend Bible college after high school. But her parents believed her Christianity would be a passing whim and told her she needed a profession to support herself. They sent her to nursing school.

Without any other Christians in her life, nursing school was a time of confusion and questioning for Bev. Had God truly called her? If so, why was life so difficult? Bev began to think God did not care about her. She fell into sin and prodigal living with the non-Christians in nursing school. Even when Bev had an opportunity to speak to Amy, she told Amy not to come visit or call. Amy kindly responded, "I won't come or call but you can't keep me from praying for you."

Two years later Bev took her state boards in Concord, New Hampshire. She decided to go to Amy's office at Child Evangelism Fellowship in the same town. Bev was dressed for riotous living that day, very different from the teenager Amy had discipled years earlier. But Amy was delighted to see Bev and welcomed her with open arms. She invited her home for dinner and talked with Bev about what she could do for God. Amy saw in Bev what Bev could not see in herself. Amy believed in Bev and was God's instrument to give her a hope and a future. Amy thought Bev would be wonderful working with troubled teens.

One year later, Bev brushed off the world and went to Bible school. In God's sovereignty Bev was called to campus ministry and work with college students. She spent twenty years with college students and then moved into ladies' ministry in mid-1990. Because of Amy's obedience to God and dramatic influence in her life, Bev has always been a pursuer of people. Just as Christ pursed Bev through Amy, it only takes one interested and committed believer to draw and disciple another. As in the case of Amy and Bev, thousands of lives can be affected by our faithfulness to disciple just one person.

For everyone, Christian or not, life is full of troubles. "Yet man is born to trouble, as the sparks fly upward" (Job 5:7). Oftentimes people expect that when we become Christians life will get easier and God will bless us. We can walk away from a sermon thinking, *If I do my best to please God, He will bless me with what I want.* Bev expected things to get easier after she came to Christ. But they didn't. God gave her a hope and eternal life but He did not make her circumstances easier. He is not the big genie in the sky. God uses all circumstances, good and bad, to work together for good to those who love God, to those who are called according to His purpose (Rom. 8:28). Why? Not to make life work out our way, but so we could be conformed to the image of His Son (Rom. 8:29) and glorify Him.

God has a sovereign purpose for our lives that is unique to us. That is why it is good to look to Him alone and not compare ourselves to other Christians, especially those Christians who seem more blessed than we are. We are told that it is unwise to compare ourselves to other believers. "For we dare not class ourselves or compare ourselves with those who commend themselves. But they, measuring themselves by themselves, and comparing themselves among themselves, are not wise. We, however, will not boast beyond measure, but within the limits of the sphere which God appointed us—a sphere which especially includes you" (2 Cor. 10:12–13).

"This Thing is From Me"

The disappointments in life are in reality only the decrees of love. I have a message for thee today. My child, I will whisper it softly in thine ear, in order that the storm clouds which appear may be gilt with glory, and that the thorns on which thou mayest have to walk be blunted. The message is but short-a tiny sentence-but allow it to sink into the depths of thine heart, and be to thee as a cushion on which to rest thy weary head: "This thing is from Me."

Hast thou never thought that all which concerns thee, concerns Me also? He that touches thee toucheth the apple of Mine eye (Zech. 2:8). Thou hast been precious in Mine eyes, that is why I take a special interest in thine upbringing. When temptation assails thee, and the "enemy comes in like a flood" I would wish thee to know that "This thing is from Me." I am the God of circumstances. Thou has not been placed where thou art by chance, but because it is the place I have chosen for thee. Didst thou not ask to become humble? Behold, I have placed thee in the very place where this lesson is to be learned. It is by the surroundings and thy companions that the working of My will is to come about.

Hast thou money difficulties? Is it hard to keep within thine income? "This thing is from Me." For I am He that possesseth all things. I wish thee to draw everything from Me, and that thou depend entirely upon Me. My riches are illimitable (Phil. 4:19). Put My promise to the proof so that it may not be said for thee, "Yet in this thing ye did not believe the Lord thy God."

Art thou passing through a night of affliction? "This thing is from Me.' I am the Man of sorrows and acquainted with grief (Isaiah 53:3) I have left thee without human support that in turning to Me thou mightest obtain eternal consolation (2 Thes. 2:16-17).

Has some friend disappointed thee? One to whom thou hadst opened thine heart? "This thing is from Me." I have allowed this disappointment that thou mightest learn that the best Friend is Jesus. He preserves us from falling, fights for us in our combats: yea, the best friend is Jesus. I long to be thy Confidant.

Has someone said false things of thee? Leave that, and come closer to Me, under My wings, away from the place of wordy dispute, for I will bring forth thy righteousness as the light, and thy judgment as the noonday (Ps. 37:6). Have thy plans been all upset? Art thou crushed and weary? "This thing is from Me." Hast thou made plans and then coming, asked Me to bless them? I wish to make thy plans for thee. I will take responsibility, for it is too heavy for thee, thou couldst not perform it alone (Ex. 18:18) Thou are but an instrument and not an agent.

Hast thou desired fervently to do some great work for Me? Instead of that thou hast been laid on one side, on a bed of sickness and suffering. "This thing is from Me." I was unable to attract thine attention whilst thou was so active. I wish to teach thee some of My deep lessons. It is only those who have learned to wait patiently who can serve Me. My greatest workers are sometimes those who are laid aside from active service in order that they may learn to wield the weapon of prayer.

Art thou suddenly called to occupy a difficult position full of responsibilities? Go forward, counting on Me. I am giving thee the position full of difficulties for the reason that Jehovah thy God will bless thee in all thy works, and in all the business of thy hands (Deut. 15:18). This day I place in thy hand a pot of holy oil. Draw from it freely, My child, that all the circumstances arising along the pathway, each word that gives thee pain, each interruption trying to thy patience, each manifestation of they feebleness, may be anointed with this oil. Remember that interruptions are divine instructions. The sting will go in the measure in which thou seest Me in all things. Therefore set your heart unto all the works that I testify among you this day. For it is your life (Deut. 31-46-47).

Found in J. Nelson Darby's Bible (Translated from French)

Next to the Bible, God speaks to us most loudly through our circumstances, because it is the most effective way to get our attention and draw us to Himself. God uses trouble to mature us to become more Christ-like. That is why the book of James says we should "count it all joy when you fall into various trials, knowing that the testing of your faith produces patience. But let patience have its perfect work, that you may be perfect and complete, lacking nothing" (James 1:2–4).

Corrie Ten Boom in *The Hiding Place* related an incident that taught her this principle. She and her sister, Betsie, had just been transferred to the worst German prison camp they had seen yet, Ravensbruck. Upon entering the barracks, they found them extremely overcrowded and flea-infested. Their Scripture reading that morning in 1 Thessalonians had reminded them to rejoice always, pray constantly, and give thanks in all circumstances. Betsie told Corrie to stop and thank the Lord for every detail of their new living quarters. Corrie at first flatly refused to give thanks for the fleas, but Betsie persisted. She finally agreed. During the months spent at that camp, they were surprised to find how openly they could hold Bible study and prayer meetings without guard interference. Several months later they learned that the guards would not enter the barracks because of the fleas.

Abraham was a man of faith who, according to Romans 4, believed God contrary to sight or conflicting circumstances when He told him that he would become the father of many nations. All the circumstances facing him from his earthly perspective (being 100 years old and his wife Sarah being many years past child bearing age) could have caused him to doubt God's word. But he did not doubt God's word; he was fully convinced that God would perform exactly what He had promised. But Abraham's faith wasn't always that strong.

As we mature in Christ, our faith should grow as Abraham's did. Early on Abram did not trust God when he was afraid that God would not protect him and Sarai in Egypt (one of the trials orchestrated by God). Abram tried to protect himself by lying (Genesis 12). As he continued in life, through the trials, he began to trust God more and more. Then God called him to the ultimate trial, to sacrifice his son, Isaac. Throughout Abraham's life God had shown Himself to be completely trustworthy. Abraham's faith grew strong and He obeyed God.

God never changes, and He works through our experiences the same way. In every situation we have two options: (1) We choose to know and believe the Word of God by faith, even when our circumstances don't make sense or seem to be the opposite of our view of what a loving God would allow in our lives or; (2) We choose not to believe His Word, and we make choices and decisions that end with consequences in our life that God never intended for us.

> *"For I know the thoughts that I think toward you,*
> *says the Lord, thoughts of peace and not of evil,*
> *to give you a future and a hope."* (Jer. 29:11)

George Mueller's book *Release the Power of Prayer* cites the prayers and circumstances of George Mueller, a man of incredible faith born in the early 1800s. Mueller was known for his unwavering faith and complete dependence on God for his own life and provision for more than ten thousand orphans without asking anyone but God to supply their needs. George Mueller's primary reason for establishing the orphanages was to show people that God and His Word can be depended upon completely.

We often react to our circumstances and ask everyone to pray for us without following some practical and biblical steps to find God's will for us in the circumstances. George Mueller had a clear understanding of how to determine the will of God. He used these steps in discerning God's will for Him on any decision he had to make.

> *"And do not be conformed to this world,*
> *but be transformed by the renewing of your mind,*
> *that you may prove what is that good and*
> *acceptable and perfect will of God."*
> (Rom. 12:2)

Steps to Know God's Will in All Circumstances

1. **Release your own will.** Get your heart into such a state that it has no will of its own in regard to a given matter. Nine-tenths of the difficulties are overcome when our hearts are ready to do the Lord's will, whatever it may be.

2. **Do not trust in feelings.** Do not leave the result to feelings or simple impression.

3. **Look to the Spirit and the Word.** Seek the will of the Spirit of God through, or in connection with, the Word of God. The Spirit and the Word must be used together. If it is of the Spirit it will be consistent with the Scriptures.

4. **Consider the circumstances.** Take into account providential circumstances. These often plainly indicate God's will in connection with His Word and Spirit.

5. **Pray for God to show you His will.** Pray that He will show you His will so you may understand it correctly.

6. **Assess your peace regarding the decision.** Thus through prayer to God, the study of the Word, and reflection, I come to a deliberate judgment, according to the best of my ability and knowledge, and if my mind is thus at peace, and continues to be after two or three more petitions, I proceed accordingly. Both in trivial matters and in transactions involving most important issues, I have found this method always effective.[1]

As you become more conscious of God working in your life, you begin to ask yourself if your decisions and actions are in harmony with the person and behavior of Christ and His Word. *Will the end result of my decision or action reflect Christ, or not?*

It is vital that we wait on God's timing and not force our circumstances. As the Old and New Testaments illustrate repeatedly, if we don't patiently wait on God's direction for our lives, we will suffer the consequences of being out of God's will.

∞ Live your life *knowing* ∞
God orchestrates your circumstances

Chapter 5 - God Orchestrates Your Circumstances

Make it Personal

1. Do you discern the sovereign hand of God in your life, or do you see things as mere occurrences?

2. What circumstances are pressing in on you right now?

3. What do you think God is expecting of you in your current situation?

4. How have you reacted to your circumstances so far? Do you tend to seek others' opinions before going to the Word of God and going to God in prayer?

5. What would you like to do differently?

6. As you respond to the circumstances in your life, are you seeing more evidence of the fruit of the Spirit in your life (love, joy, peace, patience, kindness, goodness, faithfulness, gentleness, and self-control)?

7. Oswald Chamber said,

> "Get into the habit of saying "Speak, Lord," and life will become a delight (1 Sam. 3:9). Every time circumstances press in on you, say, "Speak, Lord," and make time to listen. Hard circumstances can come for many reasons. God can use difficulties in our life as chastening. Chastening from God is meant for more than discipline—it is meant to get my attention and bring me to the point of saying, "I surrender. Speak, Lord." Think back to a time when God spoke to you."[2]

Do you remember a time when God spoke to you through His word, a sermon, a friend, or a circumstance (i.e. He gave you a hope, an encouragement to endure, clarity on a decision, etc.)?

Explain.

Chapter 6
God Called You

Are there questions in your mind you would never ask out loud? Do you wonder if this is all there is to the Christian life? Within the core of your being do you have deep longings that you cannot explain? Are you thirsty for more?

> "As the deer pants for the water brooks,
> So pants my soul for You, O God.
> My soul thirsts for God, for the living God.
> When shall I come and appear before God?"
> (Psalm 42:1–2)

If we are honest with ourselves, most of us would admit that we stay on the shoreline or at best in ankle-deep water in the Christian life. Our interactions and conversations tend to be on the surface. Our prayers are mostly asking God to get us out of or relieve our circumstances. Rarely do we pray the prayers for ourselves or others that reflect the desire to know the living God the New Testament shows us. However, just as Jesus called Peter in Luke 5 "to launch out into the deep and let down your nets for a catch of fish," He calls us to the deeper, abundant, and mature life in Christ. But how do we grow to maturity so we can fulfill God's calling on our lives?

"Therefore, brethren, be even more diligent to make your call and election sure, for if you do these things you will never stumble" (2 Pet. 1:10). The walk to maturity is outlined in 2 Peter 1. We are called to add to our original faith in Christ at salvation virtue (moral excellence), knowledge (spiritual truth from the Word of God), self-control, patience, godliness (Christ-likeness), brotherly kindness, and love (*agape* love).

We are called to grow to spiritual maturity for three primary reasons:

1. So we will know, intimately and personally know, the Lord Jesus Christ

2. To be useful in His work for us on earth

3. To have a rich inheritance in heaven

The most miserable life is that spent as a stunted baby Christian. Often we think, or are told, that if we go to church, pray, and volunteer for Christian service, as time goes on we will become mature believers. But that is rarely, if ever, true. These activities are not bad, but this is about first things first. The Bible clearly tells us that our first priority in the Christian life is our relationship and growing knowledge of Christ. The by-products or fruits of that relationship are the works related to salvation. The sad reality is that much of our church-based work for God is done in the flesh because, frankly, it is easier to be busy for Christ than to surrender our life to Him and develop a close, personal, growing relationship with our Savior. The flesh, the world, and Satan do everything to divert and preempt us from a *growing* personal relationship with Jesus Christ.

> The crisis of American spirituality, put bluntly, is Spirit versus flesh. The failure or flat refusal to abide in the mind of Christ creates duality and separation within us. We do not choose decisively between God and Mammon [material blessings], and our procrastination constitutes a decision itself. We carefully distribute ourselves between flesh and Spirit with a watchful eye on both. The unwillingness to sustain ourselves with the awareness that we are children of God causes a spiritual schizophrenia of the most frightening kind. It is not

that I am afraid to tell you who I am; I truly cannot tell you because I don't know myself who I am. I have not given the deep inner assent to my Christian identity. I am afraid of losing my life if I were to find my real self. God calls me by name, and I do not answer because I do not know my name.[1]

Colossians 3 tells us the great secret to the trial and joy-filled walk to maturity in Christ. "Set your affection on things above, not on things on the earth. For ye are dead, and you life is hid with Christ in God." At salvation we were crucified with Christ; we no longer live in the flesh, but it is Christ through the Holy Spirit who lives in us to enable us to grow on to maturity and fulfill His work uniquely through each of us. What are those things that are "above"? They are the deeper knowledge of Christ, closer fellowship with Him, experience of His resurrection power, victory over sin, the increasing evidence of godly virtues, a daily desire for His Word and prayer, and sharing Christ's salvation and resurrection reality with others. We show Christ to others by our actions, behavior, and words.

Out of this personal and intimate love relationship with the Lord Jesus Christ, we learn to discern His will for our lives, love others as we love ourselves, know what He has called us *personally* to do for Him on this earth, and respond in total trust in, and dependence on, Him to lead our lives. We are able to live transparently before others and show them Christ who is living through us (Gal. 2:20). We are no longer just living out an acceptable role in our Christian circles but living truly transformed lives that God has changed from the inside out. This is the abundant life Jesus Christ promised us in John 10:10: "The thief does not come except to steal, and to kill, and to destroy. I have come that they may have life, and that they may have it more abundantly."

∞ Live your life *knowing* ∞
God called you

Chapter 6 - God Called You

Make it Personal

1. How do you know you are a Christian (see Chapter 8)?

2. If you are a Christian briefly write your conversion experience and changes God has made in you since your salvation below.

3. In John 15 Christ talks about abiding in the Vine (Christ). The evidence of abiding is the fruit of the Spirit listed in Galatians 5:22–23a: love, joy, peace, longsuffering, kindness, goodness, faithfulness, meekness, and self-control. Have you seen evidence of the fruit of the Spirit in your life?

   Explain.

4. How would you describe your Christian experience?

   What surprises have you had?

5. In your own words explain the love of Christ toward you?

6. Based on John 14:15, 21, do you truly love Jesus Christ?

What does that look like specifically in your life?

7.   What do you believe God is calling you to do?

Where? With whom?

Chapter 7
God Calls You to Worship

"Oh come, let us worship and bow down; Let us kneel
before the Lord our Maker. For He is our God, and we
are the people of His pasture."
(Psalm 95:6–7a)

A. W. Tozer said, "To speak of the 'deeper life' is not to speak
of anything deeper than simple New Testament religion. Rather it is
to insist that believers explore the depth of the Christian evangel for
those riches it surely contains but which we are as surely missing. The
'deeper life' is deeper only because the average Christian life is tragically
shallow."[1]

The deeper Christian life, New Testament Christianity, starts with
an accurate understanding and practice of worship. God created us to
worship Him.

*"God is Spirit: and those who worship Him
must worship in spirit and truth."*
(John 4:24)

What is true biblical worship? How do we worship God in spirit
and in truth?

Spirit and truth refer to the Word of God and the human heart.
Both are vital to true worship. William Temple in his famous poem on
worship accurately portrayed worship when he said, "To worship is to
quicken the conscience by the holiness of God, to feed the mind with
the truth of God, to purge the imagination by the beauty of God, to

open the heart to the love of God, and to devote the will to the purpose of God".

Worship is
the submission of all our nature to God
It is the <u>quickening of the conscience</u> by His holiness;
the <u>nourishment of mind</u> with His truth;
the <u>purifying of the imagination</u> by His beauty;
the <u>opening of the heart</u> to His love;
the <u>surrender of will</u> to His purpose—

<u>and all of this gathered up in adoration,</u>
the most selfless emotion of which our nature is capable,
and therefore the chief remedy
of that self-centeredness
which is our original sin
and the source of all actual sin.

William Temple, 1881–1944

Worship is much more than singing songs, formal church services, or attending a service with a program that has "Worship Service" listed in the title. It is a condition of the heart, a willingness to exalt God and yield to His will. Worship is our expression of love and awe to a holy God who has given us His mercy, much more than we deserve, through our redemption in Jesus Christ. Worship is personal and deliberate. It is not self-focused but focused solely on the true and living God. Its primary purpose is to glorify God and honor and adore Him for who He is. God calls us to personal worship and corporate worship with our redeemed brothers and sisters in Christ.

What do we need to do to worship God? First and foremost, we need to have surrendered our life to Jesus Christ as Lord and Savior. We name Him our personal Redeemer. The overall pattern of our life must include the following components to be able to worship in spirit and in truth:

1. Live in obedience to His Word. Submit your will to do His will. Your loving Father will take care of you (Matthew 6).

2. Let the Holy Spirit live through you unquenched and unhindered. "He must increase, but I must decrease" (John 3:30). John the Baptist was referring to Christ in this passage. In much the same way in our Christian walk, God in us through the Holy Spirit must increase and we, our flesh, must decrease to the point of death. "For you died and your life is hidden with Christ in God" (Col. 3:3). Paul stated in Philippians 1:21, "For to me, to live is Christ, and to die is gain."

3. Take time to worship. As we grow in the knowledge of God and in our relationship to Him, our increasing desire is to worship Him. When we take time to meditate on His Word, praise Him for who He is and His love toward us, enjoy His creation, quiet ourselves in His presence, love and adore Him, and let Him be magnified, He communicates His presences to us through the act of worship.[2]

These components are to be a vital part of our worship in our daily lives and in corporate worship.

The common view of corporate worship is to attend a church worship service on Sundays and respond to whatever the program directs us to do. Sing, pray, give, and listen to the sermon when prompted. Our minds are often consumed with people, the program, our "to-do" list, or what we are gong to eat for lunch; and the painful reality is that we truly don't worship God at all.

In many cases we have volunteered to do so many things on Sundays (even at church) that we never worshipped or glorified God at all. We go home feeling like we did our "duty" and obeyed God, but there was no life in it. Why is there no life in it? Even if we are fortunate enough to be in a solid Bible teaching church and the truth component of worship is present, the spirit component is missing because we did not come prepared to worship with our hearts. God can only be worshipped in spirit and in truth. The spirit is the heart; the truth is the Word of God.

∞ **Live your life** *knowing* ∞
God calls you to worship

Chapter 7 - God Calls You to Worship

Make it Personal

1. Why does God tell us to worship Him? (Give verses to back up your response.)

2. Do you worship God in spirit and in truth on Sundays?

   If not, what would you like to change?

3. Do you worship God personally?

   If so, what does it look like?

4. Do you look forward to worshipping God or do it out of duty to God or man?

   Why?

5. Worship is often accompanied by music. That is why most old hymns of the faith contain words directly out of the Bible or combine biblical truth with the Christian experience. However, God only requires that we worship Him with our hearts (spirit) and His Word (biblical truth). Can you worship God without music?

6. If not, do the words of the music you listen to line up accurately with Scripture?

7. Scripture tells us that we will spend all eternity worshipping God. Does that seem attractive or disturbing to you?

   Why?

8. Do you see the importance of preparing your heart for Sunday worship services?

   Explain.

9. If so, do you have a current practice for preparing your heart?

   Describe.

10. What would you like to do differently to make sure you begin worshipping in spirit and in truth?

Chapter 8
How You Can Know for Sure

"The Lord is not slack concerning his promise, as some men count slackness; but is longsuffering toward us, not willing that any should perish but that all should come to **repentance.**"
(2 Peter 3:9)

Repentance means "a change of mind and heart." Biblical repentance over sin means a turning away from sin. What does repentance look like? Repentance was captured best in the radio broadcast taken from Nancy Leigh DeMoss' (10/02/2007), radio transcript www.ReviveOurHearts. com.

> "Good works will flow out of the repentant heart. If there is no fruit, there is no root. There's no evidence. There's no life. There's no growth. There's just death if there hasn't been repentance.
>
> I read a story about a notorious gangster named Mickey Cohen who attended a meeting in southern California where a famous evangelist was preaching. After the meeting this gangster expressed interest in the message. So several people talked with him and really tried to encourage him about making a decision for Christ.
>
> He didn't make a commitment to Christ at that point, but some time later another friend urged him to invite Christ into his life. At that point he professed to do so. But his life from that point on gave no evidence of repentance or any change.

He said to the friend later, "You didn't tell me I'd have to give up my work" (meaning his rackets). "You didn't tell me I'd have to give up my friends" (speaking of his fellow gangsters).

He had heard that "so and so" was a football player and someone else was a Christian actress and somebody else was a Christian Senator. So he thought he could just be a Christian gangster.

We laugh, except it's really not funny. George Gallup, the pollster, has observed that most Americans who profess to be Christians do not act significantly different from non-Christians in their daily lives. And studies after studies after studies, surveys, and polls bear this out.

Most people who profess to be Christians do not live in a way that is measurably different from those who don't claim to be Christians. We're talking about the divorce rate, views of morality, sexual experience. In category after category, the statistics are virtually the same between those who profess to be Christians and those who make no such claim.

The majority of church members in America give no visible evidence of having been born again. Something is wrong with that picture.

Think about how many church members you know—maybe it's your own experience—those who go on in their Christian life for years and years in bondage to the same sins and can't get victory. Some of them have no desire to change, make no effort to change, have no heart and no appetite for spiritual matters.

I believe the major problem is that many people sitting in our churches week after week after week have never truly been born again. They're alive physically, but they're not alive spiritually. They're religious, but they're not righteous. They profess something with their lips that they do not possess in their lives.

And I've come to believe that perhaps a huge majority of people who are members of our evangelical churches have never been converted. They're not members of *the Church*, the body of Jesus Christ.

I have no way of knowing who those people are. You have no way of knowing that. But God knows. He searches the hearts and He knows that millions and millions of those people who will be in church this Sunday, in your church and mine and in our churches across this country have made a "decision."

They've prayed a prayer. They've joined a church. They've been baptized. They serve in positions of responsibility and leadership in the church. They teach a Sunday school class. They sing on the praise and worship team. They're doing a lot of things, but many of these people have never been converted.

They're not children of God. They may be church members, but they don't belong to Christ. I think one of the big reasons for this is that for a hundred years or more now, many of our modern day evangelistic efforts have often appealed to people to join, to sign up, to walk an aisle, to do this or do that, to join the church. But they have not appealed to people to repent.

A faulty message preaching a gospel apart from repentance toward God and faith in Jesus Christ is going to produce faulty results. We can pack our churches. We've proved that we can do that. But when you begin to preach and proclaim and share the gospel, it's a whole different story.

People aren't going to line up as fast to hear that, because it requires a change of citizenship, a change of loyalty, a change of allegiance, a new king. And people don't want a new king. They want to be their own king. They don't want to repent. God has to give the gift of repentance. And apart from that repentance there is no conversion.

So we have millions of people sitting in our evangelical churches who have "accepted Christ" perhaps for what they thought He could do for them, something they thought they would gain, or something they wanted to add. Like some other world religions, they're just adding one god to their many other gods. That's not god with a capital "g." That's god with a lowercase "g." That's idolatry.

Religion for millions of evangelical Christians has become just another idol in their collection. They've accepted Christ, but they've never repented and believed the gospel. They follow Christ like the people did in John chapter 6 for what they can get out of Him.

There is no forgiveness of sins as long as you are still living under your own lordship, as long as you have not turned from the idol of self to the worship of the true and living God. **That is repentance.**

…It's saying if you are a Christian, if you have repented, if you have turned in faith to Christ, the evidence will be seen in the fact that you will perform deeds in keeping with repentance. The good works will flow out of the repentant heart.

The Scripture talks about repentance from dead works and repentance from sin. What are those dead works? A dead work is any religious act that I do that's for the purpose of gaining favor or merit with God by my own human effort. That's a dead work.

Dead works can be worship, praying, singing, tithing, good works, accepting Jesus, fasting. And I want to say again that for millions of church members in this country, "praying a prayer accepting Jesus" has been nothing more than another good work, another way they attempted to gain the favor of a holy God on their own.

It's works. It's dead. The writer to the Hebrews says in Hebrews 6:1, "We must repent of dead works" (paraphrase). We have to repent of our religion that we thought was going to save us—not just repenting of our sins. Of course that gangster needed to repent of his sins, but good church members need to repent of their dead works.

Oh, Lord, would You give us a heart that sees sin as You see it? And may we be willing to endure the grief, the sorrow, the pain of Your conviction, the conviction of Your Holy Spirit to see our sin as it really is, as a capital offense against You, to grieve it, to mourn over it in a biblical and godly way. May You give to us godly sorrow that will produce true repentance and lasting change. For Jesus' sake I pray it, amen."[1]

What are the main differences between religion (man's efforts to please God and earn a place in heaven) and Christianity (a personal relationship with God through Jesus Christ)?

Religion (Self Effort, Works)

Goal:	People reach out to God. Try to earn your way into heaven
Means:	Diligent self-effort through service & works with hopes of a reward (heaven)
Power:	Human effort through self-determination

Control: Self-motivation and self control

Results: Often results in human pride, apathy, failure, chronic guilt. Always results in eternal separation from God

Salvation through Faith In Jesus Christ (Personal Relationship)

Goal: Trust fully in God's redemptive work on the cross through Jesus Christ. Trust Jesus Christ as your Lord and Savior

Means: Confess sins, repent, yield your will to Jesus Christ (Thy will be done)

Power: After salvation, the Holy Spirit lives in us and enables us to obey God and live for Him on this earth. The power is God's power

Control: A life yielded to the Holy Spirit enables Him to control & direct our lives

Results: Love, joy, peace, humility, thankfulness, freedom to obey God's Word and will for our lives on earth. Eternal life in heaven

Knowing God Personally

God created us so that we might know Him personally.

The Bible teaches us that God love you.

"For God so loved the world that He gave His only begotten Son, that whoever believes in Him should not perish but have everlasting life." (John 3:16)

God wants you to know Him personally.

"And this is eternal life, that they may know You, the only true God, and Jesus Christ whom You have sent." (John 17:3)

But we are separated from a Holy God and His love because of our sin.

"But your iniquities have separated you from your God; And your sins have hidden His face from you, So that He will not hear." (Isaiah 59:2)

"For all have sinned, and fall short of the glory of God." (Romans 3:23)

Sin causes us to miss God's very best for our life.

Jesus said, "… I have come that they may have life, and that they may have it more abundantly" (John 10:10)

"For the wages of sin is death…" (Romans 6:23)

Sin causes us to face eternal death and judgment.

"In flaming fire taking vengeance on those who do not know God, and on those who do not obey the gospel of our Lord Jesus Christ: These shall be punished with everlasting destruction from the presence of the Lord, and from the glory of His power."
(2 Thessalonians 1:8-9)

God's Redemptive Solution

Jesus Christ died and conquered death for you.

We deserve death and judgment because of our sin, but Jesus took upon Himself the punishment for our sins, so that we could have a personal relationship with God.

"Jesus said, I am the way, the truth, and the life. No one comes to the Father except through Me." (John 14:6)

Your Response to Jesus Christ

Each of us by faith must receive Jesus Christ if we want to know God.

"But as many as received Him, He gave the right to become children of God, to those who believe in His name." (John 1:12)

"For by grace you have been saved, through faith-and that not of yourselves, it is the gift of God." (Ephesians 2:8)

What Must You do to become a Christian?

1. Acknowledge your need for a Savior. Repent of your sin by admitting that you have sinned and desire to turn from that sin. (1 John 1:8-9)

2. Believe Jesus Christ died in your place and rose again to be your Savior – providing forgiveness for your sin. (I Corinthians 15:3-4;17)

3. Surrender your life to Jesus Christ as your Lord and Savior. Invite Him to direct your life.

Sample Prayer

"Dear Lord, I want to know You personally. I am willing, with your help, to turn from my sins. Thank you for sending Jesus Christ who died in my place and rose again to be my Savior and reconcile me to a Holy God. I surrender my life to you. Come into my life and lead me. Amen."

The Result

It is important to remember that we rely upon God's Word, not our feelings, as proof of our having Christ "within us."

"That if you confess with your mouth the Lord Jesus and believe in your heart that God raised Him from the dead, you will be saved." (Romans 10:9)

"But as many who received Him, to them He gave the right to become children of God, to those who believe in His name." (John 1:12)

How to Grow in Your Relationship with God

1. Talk to God about everything – this is **prayer** (Philippians 4:6-7)

2. Listen to God by reading the bible daily – this is **bible study** (Hebrews 4:12)

3. Spend time with others who know God personally – this is **fellowship** (Hebrews 10:25)

4. Help others to know God personally – this is **disciple making** (Matt. 28:19-20)

5. Let God direct your life daily – this is **obedience** (John 14:15)

∞ **Live your life** *knowing* ∞
Christ as Your Lord & Savior

Chapter 8 - How You Can Know for Sure

Make it Personal

1. Have you repented of your sin and surrendered your life to Jesus Christ as your Lord and Savior?

If so, write your redemption story below:

2. What evidence of redemption have you seen in your life since you became a Christian?

3. What are you most thankful to God for?

4. Repentance is required for true salvation and it should be an on-going act as we are convicted of sin. As you have grown in your Christian walk, what you have repented of recently?

5. Do you read the Word of God daily?

If not, why? If so, what affect does it have on your life?

6. As you mature in Christ do you have more conviction of sin, less of a pattern of sin in your life, and more joy?

   Why?

7. How does your prayer life change when:

   a. You are routinely reading the bible?

   b. After you confess your sin to God?

8.   1 John 5:11-13 states: "And this is the testimony that God has given us eternal life, and this life is in His Son. He who has the Son has life; he who does not have the Son of God does not have life. These things I have written to you who believe in the name of the Son of God, that you may know that you have eternal life, and that you may continue to believe in the name of the Son of God." Write in your own words how you can be *confident* and *know* that you are truly redeemed in Christ?

9.   In John 10:28 Jesus said, "And I give them eternal life, and they shall never perish; neither shall anyone snatch them out of My hand." Based on Jesus words, how can you be *assured* that you will never lose your salvation?

10. In John 10:10, Jesus said, "The thief does not come except to steal, and to kill, and to destroy. I have come that they may have life, and that they may have it more abundantly." In your own words, explain the *abundant life* Jesus Christ promised for those who know Him as Lord and Savior.

Notes

Chapter 1 – God's Sovereignty
1. A. W. Pink, *The Sovereignty of God* (Grand Rapids, Mich.: Baker, 1984), 19.

Chapter 2 – God Created You
1. Ravi Zacharias, *The Grand Weaver* (Grand Rapids, Mich.: Zondervan, 2007), 14.
2. Dan B. Allender and Lisa K. Fann, *To Be Told Workbook* (Colorado Springs: WaterBrook Press, 2005), 1–3.

Chapter 3 – God Loves You
1. Oswald Chambers, *My Utmost For His Highest* (Grand Rapids, Mich.: Discovery House Publishers, 1992), March 13.
2. Ibid., May 19.

Chapter 4 – God Chose and Gifted You
1. C. S. Lewis, *The Screwtape Letters* (New York: Harper Collins, 2001), 60.
2. http//www.allaboutGOD.com/bema-seat 2008

Chapter 5 – God Orchestrates Your Circumstances
1. George Mueller, *Release the Power of Prayer* (New Kensington, Pa.: Whitaker House, 2000), 103–4.
2. Oswald Chambers, *My Utmost For His Highest* (Grand Rapids, Mich.: Discovery House, 1992), January 30.

Chapter 6 – God Called You

1. Brennan Manning, *The Importance of Being Foolish: How to Think Like Jesus* (San Francisco: HarperSanFrancisco, 2005), 127.

Chapter 7 – God Calls You to Worship

1. A. W. Tozer , *Keys to the Deeper Life* (Grand Rapids, Mich.: Zondervan, 1984), 32.

2. C. S. Lewis, *Reflections on the Psalms* (Orlando: Harcourt, Inc., 1986), 93.

Chapter 8 – How You Can Know for Sure

1. Taken from Nancy Leigh DeMoss' (10/02/2007), radio transcript www.ReviveOur Hearts.com.

Contact the Authors

Kyle Roberts – email: kyle@redeemedliving.org
phone: 813-891-6162

Bev Plimpton – email: bev@redeemedliving.org
phone: 813-480-6884

Foundation for Redeemed Living
12157 W. Linebaugh Ave., #320
Tampa, FL 33626
www.redeemedliving.org

INVITING WOMEN TO DEPTH, DIGNITY AND DELIGHT IN CHRIST

About the Authors

Kyle Roberts, a native of Florida, came to know Christ in her early 30's and has been growing in her relationship with Him ever since. Like many women of her era, prior to coming to Christ she devoted her time to her education and career. Her degrees are in engineering and business. She has been married for 23 years*. Over the past decade, Kyle has discipled and mentored women on an individual basis and worked in many church-based ladies ministries. Her heart is to help women continually grow in their intimacy with their Savior resulting in joy-filled, redemptive living.

*Including an incredible 5 year redemption story in between.

Beverly Plimpton, a native of New Hampshire, came to know Christ in her teens and was called to full-time ministry work immediately after graduating from nursing school. She spent the first 20 years in campus ministries and the past 12 years in individual and church-based ladies ministries. Bev has played a vital role in biblical counseling, mentoring, and discipling, impacting countless lives in her service to God. Her passion is to watch women grow in their walk with Christ and to invite all women to a saving knowledge of Jesus Christ.

Printed in the United States
215907BV00002B/10/P